Let's Remember....

when TEXAS

BELONGED TO

SPAIN

Written and illustrated by Betsy Warren

1981 • HENDRICK-LONG PUBLISHING COMPANY • DALLAS

CONTENTS

ISBN #0-937460-04-4

1982 copyright © by Hendrick-Long, Dallas, Texas

The FIRST SPANIARDS in TEXAS

ALONZO PIÑEDA—1519

Four Spanish ships sailed close to the shores of the Gulf of Mexico in 1519. The leader, Alonzo Piñeda (ah-LONE-zoh peen-YEH-dah), was drawing a map of the shape of the Gulf. It was the first map which showed the coastline of Texas.

Dates in subtitles indicate year of the event

Alonzo Piñeda and his men stopped where the Rio Grande flows into the Gulf. They stayed for three months to repair their ships. They visited with the Indians. These were the first white men the Indians of Texas had ever seen.

After putting up the flag of Spain, the Spaniards sailed away. For the next three hundred years, the country of Spain said that it owned the lands of Texas and Mexico. They called these lands NEW SPAIN.

4

Cabeza's travels

The EXPLORERS

CABEZA de VACA—1528

While trying to sail to Mexico, Cabeza de Vaca (cah-VAY-zah deh-VAH-cah) and a few companions from Spain were ship-wrecked on Galveston Island. Karankawa Indians rescued them.

The Spaniards stayed with the Indians. They walked with them all over South and Central Texas to find plants and animals to eat. They had to walk because there were no horses or wheels in Texas at that time.

After seven years, Cabeza de Vaca left the Indians. He made his way to Mexico where other Spaniards lived. In Mexico City, he told the rulers about the land he had seen north of the Rio Grande.

Cabeza de Vaca went back to Spain. He wrote a book about his adventures. It was the first book ever written about the land and people of Texas.

Coronado's probable route

FRANCISCO CORONADO—1540

Someone told Spanish rulers that Indians north of the Rio Grande lived in cities of gold. Captain Francisco Coronado (frahn-sees-coh coh-roh-NAH-doh) and his soldiers went to look for the cities of gold.

With 1500 horses and mules, the Spaniards rode from Mexico far to the north. Cows and sheep were also taken along to be used for food during the trip. These were the first cows, sheep, horses, and mules seen by Texas Indians.

7

Coronado and his men traveled many months. They went as far north as the Texas Panhandle. Then they went back to Mexico City without finding any gold or riches.

Coronado was sent home in disgrace. But he had done something important. Coronado had learned a great deal about the land, animals, plants, and Indians of Texas.

LUÍS MOSCOSO—1542

After claiming the land of Florida, six hundred Spaniards with horses came west to look for gold. Luís Moscoso (loo-EES mos-COH-soh) led his men to Texas. They were the first Europeans to see the land between the Red River and the Trinity River.

When their supplies ran low, Moscoso and his men traveled to Mexico City. They told the rulers that they had seen a vast land with many rivers. But they had not seen any gold.

More and more Spaniards came to explore Texas. Some of them rode horses, but many of them walked. They made maps of rivers, prairies, and mountains.

In 1650, some Spanish soldiers met Indians who greeted them with a word that sounded like TAY-SHAS. The Spaniards used this word as a name for the Indians. Sometimes they spelled it TEJAS. Later, it became the word TEXAS. TEXAS means "Friends."

Ysleta

SPANISH PRIESTS—1682

Spanish priests were sent to Texas to build missions for the Indians. The first mission was at Ysleta (ees-LAY-tuh), near El Paso. It was a church surrounded by a few straw-roofed houses built by priests and Indians. The priests asked the Indians to live in the mission. They hoped to teach them how to be farmers, Christians, and citizens of Spain.

The FRENCH in TEXAS
ROBERT LaSALLE—1685

Spanish rulers in Mexico were angry when they heard that some families from France had come to Texas. With their leader, Robert LaSalle, the French had built a fort near the coast. They put up the flag of France on the fort.

However, the French settlers were afraid of the Indians. Also, they went hungry because they did not know how to grow food. When supplies ran out, they began to fight each other. LaSalle was killed.

12

Spanish soldiers who came to chase LaSalle out of Texas found that all the French people were gone. The soldiers burned what was left of the fort.

On their way home to Mexico, the soldiers left cows and horses by the rivers they crossed. This was the beginning of great herds of wild horses and cattle in Texas.

LOUIS ST. DENIS—1714

Another Frenchman, Louis St. Denis, came to Texas from Louisiana. He wanted to sell French goods to the Spaniards in Mexico. But the Spaniards put him in a jail in Mexico City. St. Denis escaped from the jail and went back to Louisiana. He built a trading post near the Texas-Louisiana border.

The FIRST CAPITAL—1721–1773

When the Spanish heard that more and more French people were coming into Texas from Louisiana, they sent soldiers to build forts to keep the French out. They also sent priests to build missions for the Indians. The mission of Los Adaes (los ah-DAH-ace) was near the Louisiana border. It was named as the first capital of Texas, and lasted for 52 years.

MISSIONS and TOWNS

EAST TEXAS MISSIONS

Three more missions were built in East Texas near Los Adaes. Priests worked hard to teach the Indians to be craftsmen and farmers. But the Indians could not understand the ways of the white men. They often left the missions to live in the wilderness.

The ALAMO—1718

A mission called SAN ANTONIO de VALERO was built in South Texas in 1718. It was soon called the ALAMO . . . the Spanish name for the cottonwood tree. Soldiers stayed in the Alamo to protect the priests and Indians who lived there.

SAN JOSÉ MISSION—1720

The mission of San José (sahn hoe-ZAY) was built near the Alamo in 1720. It was the largest and most successful of all the missions. It held a church, carpentry and weaving shops, a mill, cattle, and large fields for crops. Indian families lived in rooms in the wide walls which were built around the mission grounds.

18

SAN ANTONIO, GOLIAD, LAREDO

In 1731, Spanish families came from the Canary Islands to settle near the Alamo. They built homes and made the town of *San Antonio*. It was the first town in Texas.

The next town was *Goliad*. In 1749, it was built close by the mission of Zuniga in East Texas. Spanish soldiers lived in the stone fort of La Bahia near Goliad and the mission.

In South Texas on the Rio Grande, the town of *Laredo* was begun in 1755.

TRAVELERS in TEXAS

PHILIP NOLAN—1791

Philip Nolan came to East Texas to find horses for the French soldiers in Louisiana. Indians gave him horses in exchange for beads, cloth, and guns.

When Nolan built a fort, Spanish soldiers came to arrest him. They were afraid he would bring more French people into Texas. While fighting the Spanish soldiers, Philip Nolan was killed.

AGUSTÍN MORFI—1799

Agustín Morfi came to Texas from Mexico. He was a priest who traveled for many months with men who were inspecting all of the Spanish missions and towns north of the Rio Grande.

When Morfi went back to Mexico, he wrote a book—the "History of Texas from 1673–1779." After Morfi's book was read in Europe, many people wanted to come to Texas to live.

EARLY SETTLERS

GIL YBARBO—1810

By the year 1800, Spanish missions in Texas were no longer used. Many of the Indians had died of diseases carried by the Europeans. The few who were left no longer wanted to live in missions.

Spanish soldiers who had lived in the forts went back to Mexico. But some families decided to stay in Texas. Gil Ybarbo (heel ee-BAHR-boh) led a group of people to build the town of Nacogdoches in 1810. They made a large stone fort where they went for safety during Indian attacks.

FILIBUSTERS and PIRATES

In the early 1800s, the people of Mexico began to fight to be free from Spain. They attacked Spanish soldiers and disobeyed the Spanish rulers.

Several groups of men wanted to separate Texas from Mexico. They were called *filibusters*. Augustus Magee and Bernardo Gutierrez (goo-tee-YEH-rehs) were filibusters. They gathered a small army and captured Nacogdoches, Goliad, and San Antonio. But the Spanish drove them out of Texas.

JEAN LaFITTE—1818

The Spanish sent ships full of gold and silver back to Spain to buy guns and equipment. Pirates often captured the ships. They took the gold and silver for themselves.

Jean LaFitte was the leader of 1000 pirates. He sailed his ships from Galveston Island into the Gulf to rob Spanish ships. Spain lost many cargoes of gold to Jean LaFitte and his pirate crews.

Dr. JAMES LONG—1819

In Louisiana, Dr. James Long gathered a small army. He was a filibuster who hoped to take Texas from Spain. He thought that Texas should be a part of the United States.

After capturing Nacogdoches and Goliad, Dr. Long needed money to buy guns and to pay his soldiers. He went to Galveston to borrow money from Jean LaFitte, the pirate. However, Dr. Long was captured by Spanish soldiers and killed.

MRS. JANE LONG—1820

Jane Long waited for her husband in a small fort near
Galveston. Her little girl and a young black servant, Kian, were
with her. All the soldiers had left the fort.

Jane Long fired a small cannon to scare away the Indians. She
and Kian gathered sea plants and caught fish for food. Mrs.
Long also gave birth to another baby girl. She stayed for a year
until some travelers passed by and told her that her husband
had been killed.

Mrs. Long went back to Louisiana but later returned to live
in Texas.

SETTLERS from the UNITED STATES
MOSES AUSTIN—1820

The Spanish governor in San Antonio did not want anyone from the United States to live in Texas. At first, he refused to see Moses Austin who had ridden a mule all the way from Missouri to see him. Moses Austin wanted to bring families to make homes in Texas. Finally, Moses convinced the governor that his settlers would help solve problems with the Indians.

When the governor gave permission for three hundred families to settle in Texas, Moses Austin went back to Missouri to find people to come.

STEPHEN F. AUSTIN—1821

At home in Missouri, Moses Austin became ill. He asked his son, Stephen, to carry out his plan of taking families to Texas. Stephen found three hundred families. He brought them to Southeastern Texas. They built cabins and farms. They called their settlement SAN FELIPE de AUSTIN. San Felipe was the first settlement made by people from the United States. Since Texas was owned by Spain, the settlers agreed to become Spanish citizens.

Now you know about some of the things that happened in Texas when it belonged to Spain.

CAN YOU REMEMBER?

1. Where did the first Spanish ships land in Texas?

   _____

2. Who brought the first horses and cows to Texas? _____

3. Why did Francisco Coronado explore Texas? _____

4. Where did Texas get its name? _____

5. What did Spanish priests try to teach the Indians? _____

   _____

6. Why did Indians leave the Spanish missions? _____

   _____

7. Name the first three towns in Texas. _____

8. What did filibusters plan to do? _____

9. Why did Moses Austin travel from Missouri to San Antonio?

   _____

10. Why did early settlers in Texas become Spanish citizens?

   _____

WHAT CAME FIRST?

Use the numbers 1,2,3,4,5, to show which event happened first.

_____ Stephen F. Austin brought settlers to Texas.

_____ Spaniards came to Texas in 1519.

_____ Dr. Long tried to capture Texas for the United States.

_____ Led by Robert LaSalle, the French built a fort in Texas.

_____ San Antonio became the first town in Texas.

MAKE THEM MATCH

Draw a line from the word to the picture that matches it.

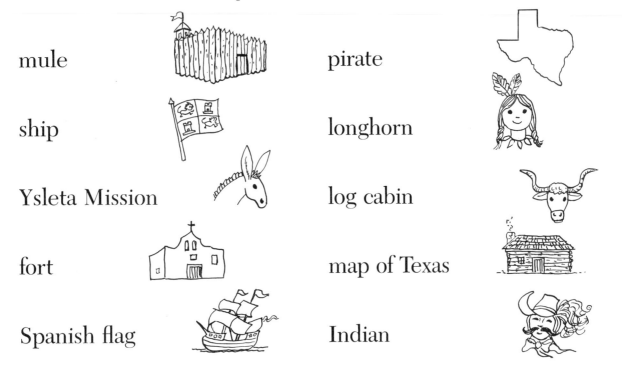

mule

ship

Ysleta Mission

fort

Spanish flag

pirate

longhorn

log cabin

map of Texas

Indian

IS IT TRUE?

Write a T before each sentence which is true.

_____ The Spaniards made Texas a part of NEW SPAIN.

_____ Indians taught the Spaniards to ride horses.

_____ Spanish explorers found gold in Texas.

_____ Waco was the first town in Texas.

_____ Spanish priests invited Indians to live in missions.

_____ The Alamo was a motel.

_____ Moses Austin rode a mule from Missouri to San Antonio.

_____ Stephen Austin brought settlers from the U.S. to live in Texas.

30

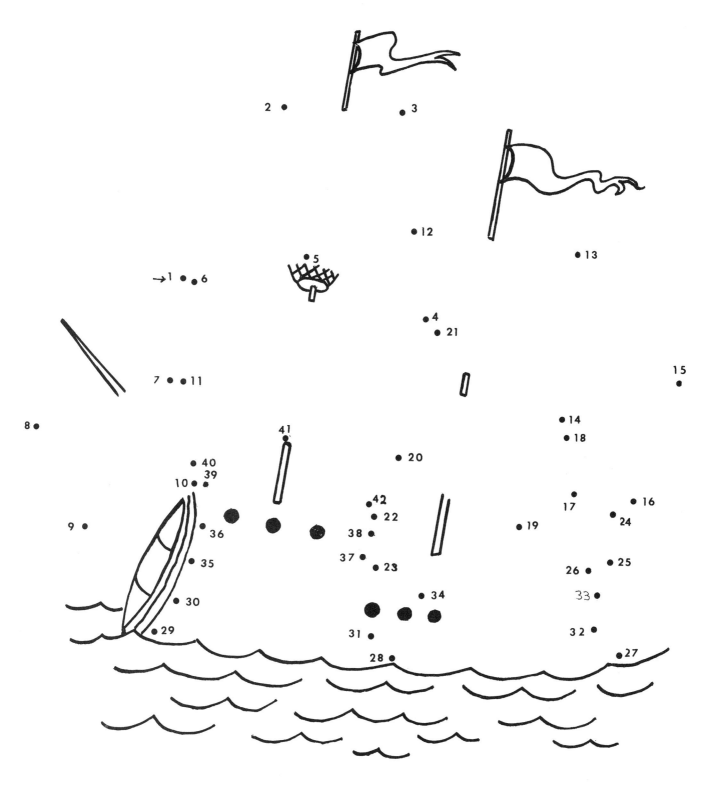

JOIN THE DOTS

. . . and see how the first Spaniards came to Texas.

CROSSWORD PUZZLE

BARTON CREEK LIBRARY
EANES ISD

ACROSS

1. _____ owned Texas for 300 years

2. Alonzo Piñeda drew a _____

3. Homemaker in a new land

DOWN

1. Spaniards sailed to Texas in _____

2. Robber of ships

3. Spanish explorers looked for _____

WORDS YOU WILL NEED

pirate
ships
gold
Spain
map
settler

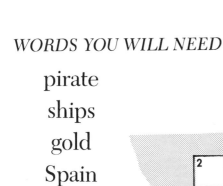

page 29 at top:
1—at mouth of Rio Grande; 2—Spaniards; 3—to find gold; 4—from the Indians; 5—to be farmers, Christians, Spanish citizens; 6—they didn't understand ways of white men; 7—San Antonio, Goliad, Laredo; 8—capture Texas from Spain; 9—to ask for land for settlers; 10—because Texas belonged to Spain.

32

page 29 at bottom:
5,1,4,2,3

page 30 at bottom:
the T goes before lines 1,5,7,8.